Traditional and Contemporary Guitar Finger-Picking Styles

BY HAPPY TRAUM

OAK PUBLICATIONS
London/New York

MUSIC SALES LIMITED
78 Newman Street, London W.1

PHOTOGRAPHS

David Gahr: 8, 11, 12, 20, 33, 38,
             43, 46, 52, 54, 60, 65, 71

Suzanne Szasz: 2

Book Design by Jean Hammons

© 1969, Oak Publications
A Division of Embassy Music Corporation
33 West 60th Street, New York 10023

Music Sales Limited
78 Newman Street
London W.1

Music Sales Australia Pty. Limited
27 Clarendon Street, Artarmon, Sydney
Australia 2064

ISBN 0-8256-0103-7
Library of Congress Catalog Number 73-93957

Printed in Great Britain by
The Camelot Press Ltd, Southampton

CONTENTS

Foreword, 5

Introduction, 6

Mance Lipscomb, 8
    Sugar Babe, 9

Mike Seeger, 12
    Fishing Blues, 13

Estil C. Ball, 16
    Pretty Polly, 17

Elizabeth Cotten, 20
    Freight Train, 21

Sibanda, 24
    Guabi Guabi, 25

Jean Bosco Mwenda, 28
    Masanga, 29

Doc Watson, 33
    Doc's Guitar, 34
    Deep River Blues, 36

John Hurt, 38
    Candy Man, 39

John Jackson, 44
    Boat's Up The River, 44

John Fahey, 46
    Poor Boy Long Ways From Home, 47
    Take A Look At That Baby, 50

Marc Silber, 52
    Fishing Blues, 53

Bert Jansch, 54
    Angie, 55

Stefan Grossman, 60
    Georgia Camp Meeting, 61

Eric Schoenberg, 65
    Dill Pickle Rag, 66

FOREWORD

When I wrote my first book, *Finger-Picking Styles for Guitar*, I had little idea as to how it would be accepted. First of all, I knew that it would only be of use to someone who already had some facility with the guitar, and that left out the beginning student. Then, I wanted the book to document, as well as teach, a particular style of guitar playing. This called for accurate transcriptions of songs and instrumentals as played by some well-known and some fairly obscure folk artists. I wondered how many people would be interested in learning, note-for-note, a piece as played by someone he has only vaguely heard of. Besides, folk music is an oral art, which loses much of its appeal when transferred to the relative sterility of the printed page.

I knew it was an important book to do, but it wasn't until *Finger-Picking Styles* was out and in its third printing within a year's time that I understood what a need there was for a book of this type. I realized then how difficult it is, even in a large urban center, to find someone to teach this style. I also saw the lack of material to be used by teachers in places where this type of playing has caught hold with such enthusiasm.

This second collection of fingerpicking pieces is to help fill that gap even more. Here I have transcribed 16 more important examples of this style, this time drawing from a broader range of performers, from the African guitarist, Mwenda Jean Bosco, to the contemporary song-writer and guitarist from England, Bert Jansch. In addition to traditional American folk artists such as Mance Lipscomb and Mississippi John Hurt, I have used some examples of traditional and original tunes arranged by city performers like John Fahey and Stefan Grossman. The songs and instrumentals in this collection, although all in the "finger-picking" style, are diverse in many ways. *Pretty Polly* and *Sugar Babe* are comparatively simple, while *Dill Pickle Rag* is extremely complex and difficult to master. *Masanga*, from Africa, is like a classical guitar piece, and *Poor Boy Long Ways From Home* is a blues in open tuning. There are many different techniques to be learned in these pages, and studying them will teach you more than simply another guitar piece to play. They will give you insight into traditional music and, hopefully, the people who make the music. They should open many doors for you, leading you into new areas of listening and playing.

It is not necessary to have studied *Finger-Picking Styles for Guitar* before attempting this collection. This is meant to be a companion volume, rather than a more advanced method book. It is arranged similarly to the other, starting with the easier pieces and gradually building in complexity and technical difficulty. You will, however, need to have a basic understanding of the finger-picking technique, since that aspect of instruction is not included here. If necessary, you may have to study the chapter *Starting To Pick* in the other book.

I am sure that if you love the finger-picking style of guitar playing as much as I do, you will find this book of songs and instrumentals as challenging and as exciting to learn as I did in collecting and transcribing them.

I would like to thank Stefan Grossman and Ricky Schoenberg for providing transcriptions for their songs, *Georgia Camp Meeting* and *Dill Pickle Rag*; and Jack Baker, of the Fretted Instruments School of Folk Music in New York City, for his transcriptions of *Doc's Guitar* and *Deep River Blues*. Thanks, too, to Dick Weissman, whose large record collection was of great value in my research of this material. —Happy Traum

INTRODUCTION

Among students of folk guitar, the most popular and exciting style of playing is undoubtedly that style usually called "Travis picking," but also variously known as "two-finger picking," "three-finger picking," "Cotten picking," and just plain "picking." Whether swinging along with a bouncy ragtime tune or quietly rippling behind a pretty ballad, the sound is distinctive. It has a groove all its own, and once you've heard it you can't mistake the steady thump of the bass strings and the bright syncopation of the treble. It has become the goal towards which so many aspiring instrumentalists work, and once it is perfected there are endless possibilities for growth and exploration.

The basis of traditional finger picking styles is the "independent thumb," keeping a steady (usually 4/4) beat regardless of what the other fingers are doing. The first (or first and second) finger picks out the melody notes, sometimes playing them *on* the beat along with the bass, and sometimes *off* the beat, by putting the note between beats. The syncopated note can come either before or after the bass note. It is this syncopated melody against the steady bass that gives it such a distinctive (and swingy) sound.

This particular style of playing seems to have started among Negro folk musicians just after the turn of the century, probably in imitation of the ragtime piano styles being played then, with its stride bass and free right hand syncopations. The fact that it was primarily a Negro style did not stop it from transcending racial barriers, and many of the white folk musicians who play this way learned directly from Negro guitarists. The interplay between white and Negro folk music was (and still is) a dominant force in creating the American folk styles as we know them, and the picking styles that concern us in this book are notable examples of that fact.

In order to help the student learn just what is happening in traditional picking styles, I have transcribed several outstanding examples from the recordings of some of the best and most influential exponents of this style. It is hoped that the student will learn these transcriptions not merely to imitate, but to be able to get *inside* the style and develop his own creative approach to picking. Among the numbers of fine folk guitarists, each one has a distinctive, unique way of playing.

It is not necessary to play every piece here note for note exactly as transcribed. It is much more important to get the feel of the style, and play the piece your own way. Try to get to concerts as much as possible to see and hear these artists in person. After all, this is a living and vital art form, and the printed page is a poor substitute for the real thing.

Listen to records! Many songs transcribed in this book have been taken from recordings, noted with the comments about the piece. More important than listening to the particular tune at hand, though, is to listen to many other things by the same person, so that you can get a real feeling for his work; his singing and playing style, his "sound," his culture, and his personality. Folk music is an oral tradition still, even if you are learning only indirectly, through the person's recordings.

Use the transcriptions as a guide to enable you to figure out passages that you can't get by just listening. Always supplement the transcription by listening to the record, because there are things for which we have no printed language.

Note on reading the tablature:

The guitar tablature provided here is a substitute for (or a supplement to) the standard musical notation. The six lines represent the six strings of the guitar, with the bass E as the bottom line.

Ex. A

The number on the line is the fret at which the left hand finger stops the string. Thus, a C chord would be shown as

Ex. B

Two notes tied together with the letter H in between indicates a "hammer-on":

Ex. C

P is a "pull-off" (left hand pluck):

Ex. D

S is a slide from one fret to another, or to a fret from an optional point below it:

Ex. E

~ indicates a "choked" or "slurred" note, produced by stretching the string with the finger that is fretting it, thus raising the note, making a whining blue-note effect. A note can be raised a half tone or more this way.

Occasionally it is necessary to notate which right hand finger picks a string, and these are designated by the letters T (thumb), I (index), M (middle) and R (ring).

Mance Lipscomb

A Texas musician who has spent most of his life working as a farmer and sharecropper, Mance Lipscomb has learned (in more than fifty years of living and making music) hundreds of songs and can play a multitude of guitar styles; blues, rags, ballads, breakdowns, and religious songs. He is also a marvelous raconteur, and can keep an audience (or friends) amused for hours with his tales, anecdotes, and revealing commentary on southern Negro life during the past half-century.

Sugar Babe was transcribed from *Mance Lipscomb, Texas Sharecropper and Songster*, Arhoolie Records (F1001).

SUGAR BABE

© Tradition Music. Used by permission.

All I want my baby to do
Make five dollars and give me two,
Sugar Babe, It's all over now.

Went down town and bought me a rope,
Whipped my baby 'til she Buzzard Lope*
Sugar Babe, It's all over now.

Sugar Babe, what's the matter with you?
You don't treat me like you used to do.
Sugar Babe, It's all over now.

Went downtown and bought me a line,
Whipped my baby 'til she changed her mind,
Sugar Babe, Sugar Babe, It's all over now.

*According to the record notes, the Buzzard Lope is a "strutting dance step; in this context to make her get a move on."

SUGAR BABE – Mance Lipscomb

Mike Seeger

Mike Seeger is one of the most respected performers of traditional music, both for his profound knowledge of American folk music and for his versatility as a performer (he plays guitar, banjo, fiddle, autoharp, mandolin, and harmonica, all well). He has been a solo performer and a collector in the field, but is best known as one of the New Lost City Ramblers.

Fishing Blues was originally heard by city audiences when Folkways re-issued it on their *Anthology of American Music* (Songs No. 4; FP 253) sung and played by Henry Thomas. It has since been recorded by The Lovin' Spoonful, the Kweskin Jug Band, and others. Mike Seeger's version is transcribed here as an excellent example of traditional finger-picking style. It is from his Vanguard album (VRS-9150). Mike plays this in the D position, with the capo on the fifth fret which makes the actual key G. (Of course, if you want to play along with the record, the capo is optional. You can place it at any fret, or play without it, depending on your vocal range.)

FISHING BLUES

Guitar arrangement by Mississippi Mike Seeger.
Used by permission.

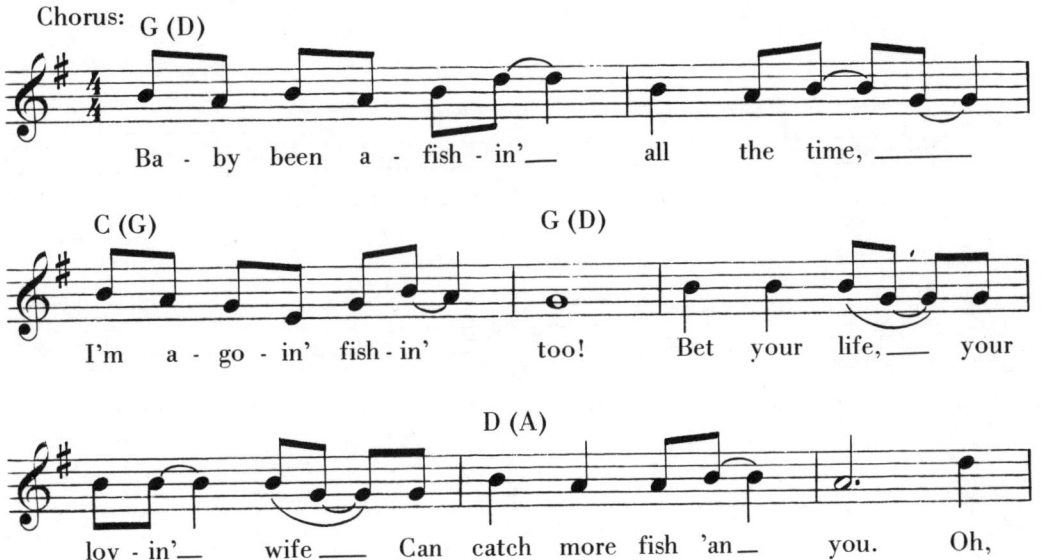

Chorus

Went down the road about four o'clock
Spied them catfish shimmying around.
Got so hungry didn't know what to do,
I'm gonna catch me a catfish too.

Chorus

Put on the skillet, put on the lid,
Mama's gonna cook a little shortnin'
  bread.

Chorus

FISHING BLUES – Mike Seeger

FISHING BLUES - Mike Seeger

Estil C. Ball

Estil C. Ball lives high in the mountains in Rugby, Virginia, and ballads and folk songs have been sung in his family for generations. He was recorded in the late 'thirties by Alan Lomax for the Library of Congress and more recently on two albums of songs collected by Lomax on Atlantic and Prestige records. Estil Ball and his wife (on accordion) make tapes of gospel songs which are played each week on several radio stations in the South.

Two albums are being made of his singing and playing; one, of gospel songs, on County Records; the other, recorded by John Cohen, will be issued on Folkways.

Of all the "murder ballads," *Pretty Polly* is probably the best known and most widely sung. Every traditional singer seems to have his own special variant of the song, although the story always remains the same. The strange modal quality of the melody has made most people adapt it to the banjo, which can be put into a special tuning to fit the song. Estil Ball plays his guitar almost like a banjo, except that it is in a straight major chord throughout. Unlike most of the finger-picking songs in this book, the melody is played with the thumb on the bass strings.

There is a kind of "pattern-picking" throughout the song, broken up by the brief melodic passages which answer the singing. Fret the E chord, only occasionally shifting your fingers to make the notes you need that are not in the chord.

This version was transcribed from *Southern Journey, Volume 9—Bad Man Ballads*, collected by Alan Lomax, Prestige International (INT 25009).

PRETTY POLLY

© Estil C. Ball. Used by permission.

She got up behind him and away they did go (2x)
Over the hills to the valley so low.

They went a little farther and what did they spy (2x)
A new dug grave with a spade lying by.

He stabbed her through the heart, her heart's blood did flow (2x)
And into the grave Pretty Polly did go.

He threw something over her and turned to go home (2x)
Leaving nothing behind him but the girl there to moan.

Gentlemen and ladies, I bid you farewell (2x)
For killin' Pretty Polly will send my soul to Hell.

PRETTY POLLY – Estil C. Ball

PRETTY POLLY - Estil C. Ball

Elizabeth Cotten

The singing and picking of Elizabeth Cotten should be well-known to anyone interested in traditional guitar styles. Her playing is strong and solid with a very individual sound. Perhaps it is because she plays the guitar left-handed, with the guitar held upside down, that gives her playing such a distinctive style (her index finger picks the bass strings, and her thumb plays the treble melody line). That is certainly part of it, but there is more to it than that. She is a fine musician with many years of experience not just with the guitar but with life. It shows in the strength of her music.

Freight Train is Libba Cotten's most well-known song. It has been recorded many times, has been sung in hundreds of concerts and picked by countless young guitarists. It was even a hit song once, although Mrs. Cotten never received the monetary benefits from it.

I used *Freight Train* in *Finger-Picking Styles for Guitar* to illustrate a style called "pattern-picking." Here it is in its original, and much more important, form. As recorded by Elizabeth Cotten on her Folkways album *Negro Folksongs and Tunes* (FG 3526).

FREIGHT TRAIN

© Elizabeth Cotten.
Used by permission.

When I'm dead and in my grave,
No more good times here I'll crave,
Place the stones at my head and feet
And tell them I've gone to sleep.

When I die, Lord, bury me deep,
Way down on old Chestnut Street,
So I can hear old Number Nine
As she comes rolling by.

When I die, Lord, bury me deep,
Way down on old Chestnut Street,
Place the stones at my head and feet
And tell them I've gone to sleep.

FREIGHT TRAIN - Libba Cotten

FREIGHT TRAIN - Libba Cotten

Sibanda

Guabi Guabi has been recorded several times by American folksingers, but very few people, unfortunately, have had the opportunity to hear the original. It was recorded in the early 'fifties by Hugh Tracy, the well-known authority on African music, and issued on a record called *Guitars of Africa* (Decca Record Company Ltd., London, England LF 1170). *Guabi Guabi* and *Masanga* are two of eight beautiful examples of African guitar playing transcribed from this record. If you cannot get the original, listen to Jack Elliott's *Guabi Guabi* (Vanguard VRS-9151) or Jim Kweskin's (Vanguard VRS-9188).

According to the album notes Sibanda has lived all his life in the native quarters of Bulawayo and is a member of the Zulu/Nde-ele tribe.

Guabi guabi is a local children's game in which you offer someone a present or something nice to eat saying, "Guess, guess what I've got," giving them a quick glance and then hiding it again. He is teasing his girl, making her guess what he has behind his back, buns, sweets, or bananas.

Sibanda often gives the song a strong rhythmic quality by strumming chords (as opposed to single bass notes) while he picks out the melody in the treble. When the chord is *on* the beat it is played with the thumb. When it is on the *off*-beat it is a brush in an upward direction with the index finger. Although there are specific chords in the transcription it is never really specific when actually played. Just brush down approximately where the designated notes should be, and don't worry too much about the exact notes of the chord.

I am indebted to Andrew Tracey of The African Music Society, for his assistance in accurately transcribing this material. If you are unable to obtain "Guitars of Africa," it has been republished along with a lot more African guitar music on two 12" LPs in "The Music of Africa Series," available from the African Music Society, Box 138, Roodepoort, Transvaal, South Africa, at $5.95 U.S.

GUABI GUABI

By Sibanda.
From "Guitars of Africa," Decca LF 1170.
Collected by Hugh Tracey.

Guabi guabi gu - zwa ngle nto - mbya mi, I - hlal e - nka-

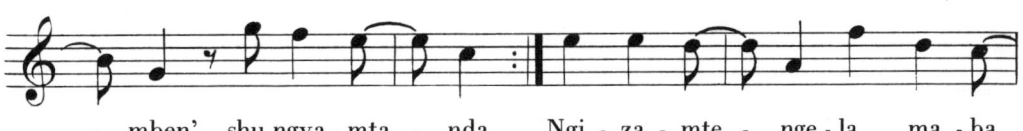
-mben', shu ngya - mta - nda. Ngi - za - mte - nge - la ma - ba

-nzi, I - zi - wi - chi, le ba - na - na, Ngi - za - mte

-nge - la ma - ba - nzi, I - zi - wi - chi le ba - na - na -.

GUABI GUABI GUZWA NGLE NTOMB YAMI,
Hear Guabi Guabi, I have a girlfriend,

IHLAL ENKAMBEN', SHU NGYAMTANDA.
She lives at Nkamba, sure I love her.

NGIZAMTENGELA MABANZI, IZIWICHI LE BANANA.
I will buy her buns, sweets and bananas.

All vowel sounds pronounced open and clear exactly as in Italian. (This note applies to Masanga too.)

The 'NG' sounds to be pronounced soft as in SINGING, not as in FINGER.

'HL' is pronounced exactly as 'LL' in Welsh, i.e. put your tongue in position to make an L and breathe past it before releasing the L.

Make the linked (‿) words continuous, as if they were one word.

GUABI GUABI - Sibanda

GUABI GUABI - Sibanda

Jean Bosco Mwenda

Masanga is one of two songs on *Guitars of Africa* sung and played by Jean Bosco Mwenda, a member of the Sanga tribe of the Congo. His singing and especially his guitar improvisations are evidence of a profound and exciting musical talent. Like most folk musicians he is completely self-taught, but his guitar playing doesn't fall into traditional categories. Influenced heavily by Brazilian music which he heard on records and combined with an African tribal heritage Bosco's music is inventive and original.

Masanga has the feeling of a western classical guitar piece. The theme is played in the treble, the bass filling in with harmony notes (not providing the steady beat as in most folk styles discussed in this book). Throughout the piece there is an interesting feeling of counterpoint and invention—you feel that Bosco could go on and on creating new and different variations. At one point the lead switches to the bass with a wonderful rhythmic change breaking up the regularity of the theme which you are just beginning to get used to.

Bosco capos at the fifth fret and plays in G, which makes the actual key C. This gives the piece a lovely light sound.

The words are in Swahili—"A woman without a husband is like a bicycle without a lamp."

There is an interesting article on Jean Bosco Mwenda in *Sing Out!* April-May 1964 (Vol. 14, No. 2) by Pete Seeger.

MASANGA

By Jean Bosco Mwenda.
From "Guitars of Africa," Decca LF 1170.
Collected by Hugh Tracy.

MASANGA – Jean Bosco Mwenda

MASANGA – Jean Bosco Mwenda

MASANGA – Jean Bosco Mwenda

Doc Watson

Doc Watson's technical virtuosity has been admired by countless young guitar pickers across the country. He is best known for his flat-picking—lightning fast and incredibly accurate—but his finger-picking is some of the best that can be found. He plays Merle Travis style, muting the bass strings with the heel of his right hand while his index fingers pick out the melody with just the right touch of jazz influence to make it swing.

Doc Watson is more than a fine guitarist. To quote A. L. Lloyd: "... it is generally recognized that there's not another performer of American folk music to touch him for power, warmth, genuine feeling, and versatility both as a singer and instrumental virtuoso."*
I think anyone who hears him could not help but agree.

Ticklin' the Strings (sometimes called *Doc's Guitar*) is one of Doc's show-stoppers. He picks it at an unbelievable speed. You'll have to start slowly, gradually increasing your tempo. Except for the fast pace, it is not a very difficult piece.

Note the change in the right hand in the fourth and fifth measures before the ending.

To play with Doc, capo the 4th fret.

This piece can be heard on *Doc Watson* — Vanguard (VRS-9152) and *Country Music and Bluegrass at Newport* (VRS-9146) from which it was transcribed by Jack Baker of The Fretted Instruments School of Folk Music, New York City.

*From the liner notes on his album Home Again! — Vanguard VRS-9239 (mono), VSD-79239 (stereo).

DOC'S GUITAR

© Doc Watson. Used by permission.

DOC'S GUITAR - Doc Watson

DEEP RIVER BLUES

Deep River Blues is one of Doc Watson's most requested songs. He uses his Travis style picking both for the accompaniment and the instrumental breaks, which gives the song a light, bouncy feeling.

Here are some chord positions you'll need to know, in case you're not already familiar with them:

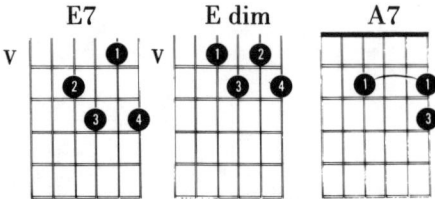

Doc gets a special kind of effect by using a "double-thumbing" technique now and then in the instrumental break. The right hand is marked in these measures.

To play along with the record, capo the 2nd fret.

Transcribed by Jack Baker from *Doc Watson*, Vanguard (VRS-9152, stereo VSD-79152).

© Doc Watson. Used by permission.

Let it rain, let it pour, Let it rain a

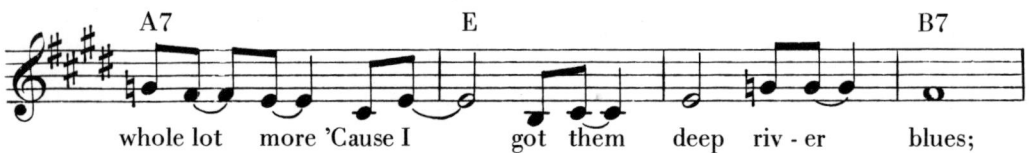
whole lot more 'Cause I got them deep riv-er blues;

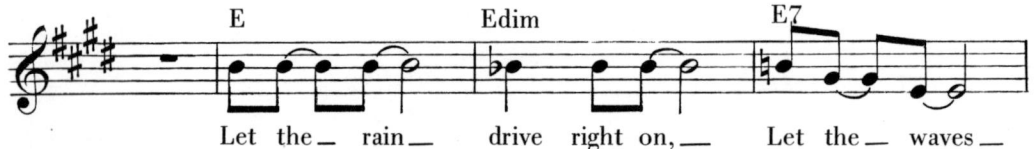
Let the rain drive right on, Let the waves

sweep a-long 'Cause I got them deep riv-er blues.

    My old gal's a good old pal   Give me back my old boat
    And she looks like a water fowl   I'm gonna sail if she'll float
    When I get those Deep River Blues;   'Cause I got them Deep River Blues;
    Th' aint no one to cry for me   I'm goin' back to Muscle Shoals
    And the fish all go out on a spree   Times are better there I'm told
    When I get those Deep River Blues.   'Cause I got them Deep River Blues.

DEEP RIVER BLUES - Doc Watson

John Hurt

When John Hurt died in 1966 he left behind him many thousands of sorrowing friends. Anyone who met him, indeed anyone who heard him play in person, could not help but feel that this man was his friend and was saddened to see him go. His guitar style was similar to his personality—quiet, simple, direct, gentle.

Since 1963, when he was sought out and "rediscovered," John Hurt had been picking and singing in colleges, coffee houses, festivals, and concert halls all over the country.

CANDY MAN

© 1963, Wynwood Music Company.
All rights reserved. Used by permission.

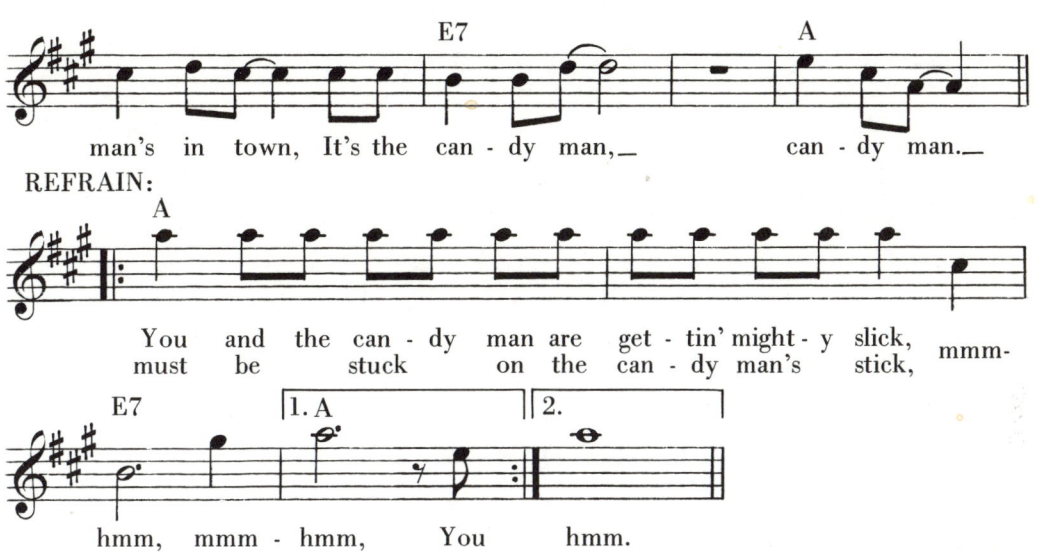

He's got a stick of candy just nine inches long,
He sells it fast as (a) hog chews his corn
He's a candy man, candy man.

You all heard what Sister Jones said,
She always takes the candy stick to bed.
It's the candy man.

Refrain:

Here's a stick of candy don't melt away,
It just gets better so the ladies say,
He's a candy man, candy man.

Refrain:

CANDY MAN – John Hurt

Candy Man is one of Mississippi John Hurt's best "picking" pieces, and the one that guitar students most want to learn.

The first part (accompaniment) is played while the song is sung. You'll notice that the bass line in this song is not the usual alternating bass pattern, but is less regular, with bass runs and harmonies adding interest throughout the song. The E7 chord in the 6th measure of the "accompaniment" and the 9th measure of the "break" should be played this way:

The instrumental break is a little more difficult, involving several positions high on the neck. The first is a slide to an E chord on the 9th fret:

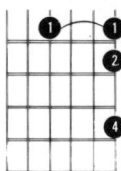

The next is an A on the 9th fret, but using the open D string as a bass note, giving a drone effect:

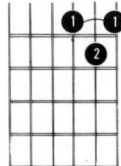

The chords that follow are D, A and E7:

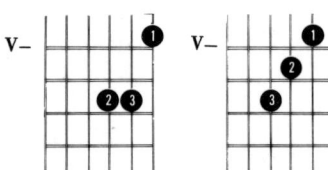 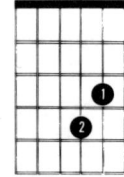

The E7 in the fourth measure from the end should be played this way:

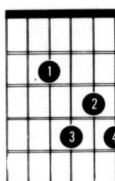

Candy Man can be heard on *Mississippi John Hurt* (Piedmont) and *Mississippi John Hurt/Today* (Vanguard VRS-9220).

CANDY MAN - John Hurt

41

CANDY MAN - John Hurt

John Jackson

Born and raised in Virginia, John Jackson now lives in Fairfax, not far from Washington, D.C., where he is very popular among the folk singing community in that area. He came from a musical family (his father played guitar, his mother accordion) and started playing the guitar at the age of four. He has a large repertoire of songs of all kinds including country and pop songs as well as Negro blues, dance tunes, and ballads.

BOAT'S UP THE RIVER

© 1969 by John Jackson.
Used by permission.

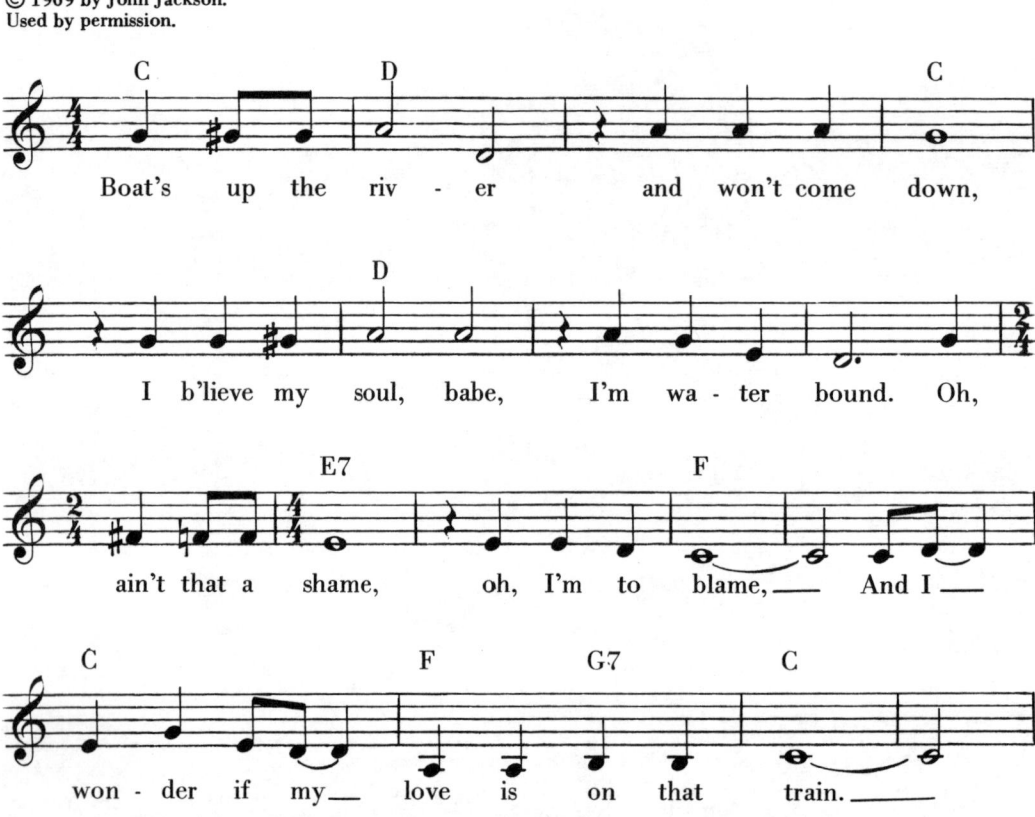

Boat's Up The River was transcribed from his album *Blues and Country Dance Tunes From Virginia*, Arhoolie Records (F1025). It's a simple tune, similar to *Freight Train*, but with an interesting chord change from C to C# to D. To play it, slide the C chord position up one fret (C#), then one more (D).

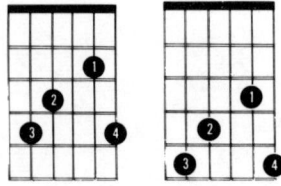

Be careful not to play the open 3rd string with these chords. You can damp (kill) the sound of that string by touching it lightly with your 2nd finger (the one fretting the 4th string).

BOAT'S UP THE RIVER - John Jackson

John Fahey

John Fahey's first three recordings for a small West Coast label (Tacoma) have gained him a growing and devoted following among city audiences. He is an instrumentalist who uses blues and fingerpicking techniques in unusual compositions and extended arrangements of traditional tunes. His use of open tunings, modal scales and harmonies, slide guitar styles, etc. add a feeling of exploration and experimentation that is rare among "folk" guitarists.

He now records for Vanguard Records.

Poor Boy Long Ways From Home is done in an open D tuning. Lower your 6th string one whole tone to a D. (This should be one octave lower than the open 4th string.) Now tune the 1st string down one whole tone (so it's an octave higher than the 4th string). Next, lower the 3rd (G) string one half step to an F#. (You can check it against the 4th string, fourth fret.) Lower your 2nd string one whole step to an A (one octave higher than the open 5th) and you are in D tuning – D A D F# A D.

This is a simple tune but it will give you a good feel for the tuning. It is instructive in building variations on a theme; try to build some of your own.

Transcribed from *John Fahey/Blind Joe Death* (Tacoma C1002).

POOR BOY LONG WAYS FROM HOME

© John Fahey. Used by permission.

POOR BOY LONG WAYS FROM HOME - John Fahey

VARIATION I

POOR BOY LONG WAYS FROM HOME – John Fahey

VARIATION II

TAKE A LOOK AT THAT BABY

Take A Look At That Baby is a ragtime piece and fun to play. Its style is similar to many other songs and if you can learn this it won't be difficult to pick up *Salty Dog, Rag Mama, Ella Speed,* and even *Alice's Restaurant.* It was transcribed from *Death Chants, Breakdowns, and Military Waltzes* — John Fahey Vol. II (Tacoma C1003). If you want to play along with the record, put your capo on the fourth fret.

© John Fahey. Used by permission.

TAKE A LOOK AT THAT BABY - John Fahey

Marc Silber

Here's that old *Fishing Blues* again, this time all dressed up with a new look. Marc Silber, a talented singer, guitarist, songwriter, wanderer, and fixer of old Martins, reworked the tune with a moving bass line that keeps your left hand fingers working pretty hard.

FISHING BLUES

© 1969 Embassy Music Corporation.
Used by permission.

53

Bert Jansch

Bert Jansch is one of a "new wave" of English folksingers and guitarists (Jansch is actually Scottish, but based in London) who are using traditional music as a basis for creating their own songs and styles. British and Scottish ballads, American blues and rags, Eastern modes, are all used in the creation and the effect is often very powerful. More important is the potential, for one feels this is only the beginning of many new forms of musical experimentation. Jansch is now a member of the well-known British group Pentangle.

ANGIE

Angie was written by guitarist Davey Graham, whose reputation (along with Jansch's) has gotten to this side of the Atlantic before he has. The song was first heard in this country as an instrumental by Simon & Garfunkel on their *Sounds of Silence* album (Columbia CL2469), and later on Bert Jansch's *Lucky Thirteen* (Vanguard VRS-9212), from which it is transcribed here.

There are four distinct parts to this piece. The theme (part A) is the most important, and repeats after each section. The treble melody is played against a constant bass pattern:

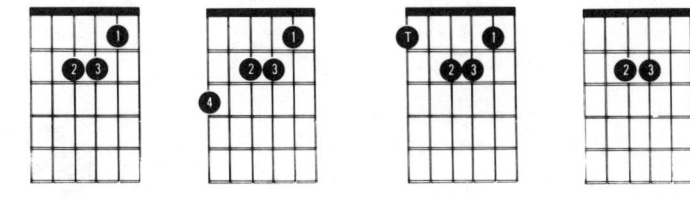

A wiggley line next to a group of notes (as in the eighth measure) represents a *roll* in which the right hand fingers brush down across the strings in rapid succession, a technique known as the *rasguado* in classical guitar language.

An x over a chord (section D) means that that chord is strummed and then immediately damped (stopped from sounding). This is done by strumming down across the strings with nails of your right hand, followed by the open hand damping the strings.

ANGIE - Bert Jansch

© 1965, Young Music Limited. Used by permission.

ANGIE - Bert Jansch

ANGIE - Bert Jansch

58

ANGIE - Bert Jansch

Stefan Grossman

Stefan Grossman is a young guitarist from New York with a vast knowledge of the blues and the people who have made the blues over the years. He studied with Rev. Gary Davis, and then went on to develop that and many other blues guitar styles, learning from his large collection of records and tapes. Being a versatile musician, Stefan went on to play rock guitar with the Fugs, the Chicago Loop, and other groups. He is now in England, where his reputation has spread quickly, keeping him in constant demand in folk clubs, concert halls, and recording studios. Stefan Grossman is the author of *The Country Blues Guitar* (Oak).

GEORGIA CAMP MEETING

Georgia Camp Meeting is one of the most difficult pieces in this book, although it is by no means impossible to play. Stefan arranged it so that in addition to the melody there is an interesting and constantly moving bass line. In order to achieve this, he uses many positions high on the neck, at the same time utilizing open strings as much as possible.

The difficulty lies in the fact that in several passages there is no chord to hold down as a basis for the left-hand fingering. In the first two measures, for example, there is a good deal of left-hand movement until the third and fourth measures when you fret a C chord and a G chord. The small numbers next to the notes (not the tablature) indicate left-hand fingering.

© Stefan Grossman. Used by permission.

61

GEORGIA CAMP MEETING – Stefan Grossman

GEORGIA CAMP MEETING – Stefan Grossman

GEORGIA CAMP MEETING - Stefan Grossman

Eric Schoenberg

Dill Pickle Rag, an old ragtime piano piece, has recently been used as a fiddle, mandolin, or banjo showpiece. Doc Watson flat-picks it on the guitar in his inimitable way. Now Eric Schoenberg, a young guitarist from New Jersey, has made an arrangement for solo guitar with all of the complexities of the original piano arrangement—harmonies, counterpoint, walking basses. It's worth taking the time to learn this because the ideas can be used to create other pieces like it. There are dozens of rags, fiddle tunes, etc. that could use a good guitar arrangement.

DILL PICKLE RAG

Here are some chord positions that will help you. The small circled number next to the chord is for identification in the music.

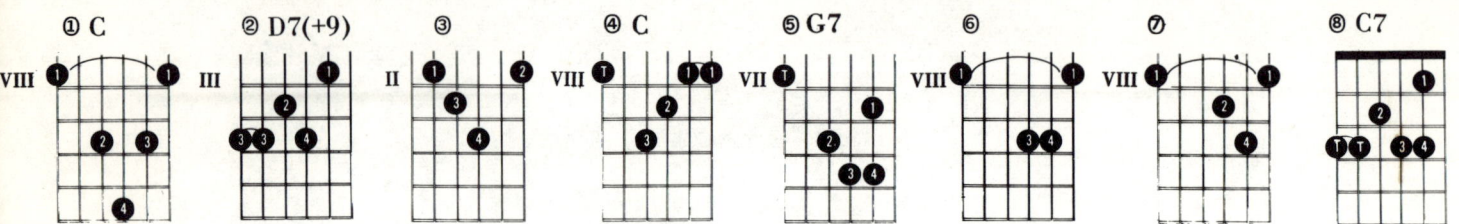

© Ricky Schoenberg. Used by permission.

DILL PICKLE RAG – Eric Schoenberg

DILL PICKLE RAG - Eric Schoenberg

DILL PICKLE RAG - Eric Schoenberg

69

DILL PICKLE RAG - Eric Schoenberg

Yank Rachel   Mississippi John Hurt   Skip James   Elizabeth Cotten   Doc Reese   Sleepy John Estes

MARCH 1975